THE GOLDEN RULE OF SUCCESS

What and How of Success from the People who Achieved it

Max Lee

For everyone that ever had a dream

CONTENTS

PREFACE

"Two roads diverged in a yellow wood,

And sorry I could not travel both

And be one traveler, long I stood

And looked down one as far as I could

To where it bent in the undergrowth;"

Success is sought by almost every man and woman in the world and yet so few actually achieve it. Why is this? I believe it is because they don't know what the problem is, they don't know what success is, what it is constituted of, and therefore they can't even start the journey.

"Then took the other, as just as fair,

And having perhaps the better claim,

Because it was grassy and wanted wear;

Though as for that the passing there

Had worn them really about the same,"

Successful people know what success is, and they go for it. And they never look back, as they tread the path one step at a time.

"And both that morning equally lay

In leaves no step had trodden black.

Oh, I kept the first for another day!

Yet knowing how way leads on to way,

I doubted if I should ever come back."

A good start is half the battle. By taking that first step, you're already ahead the majority of people. Then, it is a journey of no return.

I shall be telling this with a sigh

Somewhere ages and ages hence:

Two roads diverged in a wood, and I—

I took the one less traveled by,

And that has made all the difference.

When you tell something with a sigh, you make your influence felt in the world, which is the state of success. Being able to make a difference. But it was the choice at that very beginning which led to all this.

Now, imagine that you are the one standing at the **"two roads diverged in a yellow wood."** What would you do? Which choice would you make?

Bill Gates, often the richest person on Earth, said, **"I believe that if you show people the problems and you show them the solutions they will be moved to act."**

Do you want to achieve success?

And be happier and enjoy life more?

This book will show you the problem, and it will show you the solutions, so that you will be moved to act.

The fact is that most people are not aware of what the problem is; they don't know what success is, what it is constituted of, and therefore nothing gets done. Nothing can get done. They're at a standstill, quite literally, and they may not even realize it.

The first step is to identify the problem. What is success? If you want to know what success is, go to the people who actually achieved it, because they knew success, by the virtue of being successful. Luckily for us, many of them have been willing to show us what the problem is.

The first section, *Success: What is it?* contains numerous quotes from the most successful people who ever walked the Earth, both past and present, to drill down on what success is.

The second step is to get the solutions. To get the solutions, go directly to the answer keys — the successful people. Luckily for us, once again, many of them have been willing to show us the solutions.

The second section, *Success: How to get it?* contains a handsome amount of quotes from the most successful people who ever were present, to get all the ingredients, and all the recipes, to success.

Then, will you be moved to act, and to achieve success? *Yes! You will, indeed!* But, you need all the help you can get, right? That's why this book includes a section bursting with motivational quotes from highly successful people, for those times when you feel down and wouldn't mind a good kick, to uplift you on your way.

With this three-pronged approach to success — theory, practice, and motivation — success is, I believe, just a choice away — a willingness to follow your heart.

Godspeed,

Max Lee

The Golden Rule of Success

What and How of Success from the People who Achieved it

SUCCESS: *What is it?*

1

"Success is the only motivational factor that a boy with character needs."

Woody Hayes (1913 - 1987)

Football player

2

"Every success is usually an admission ticket to a new set of decisions."

Henry A. Kissinger (1923 -)

Former United States Secretary of State

3

"You have reached the pinnacle of success as soon as you become uninterested in money, compliments, or publicity."

Thomas Wolfe (1900 - 1938)

Author

4

"Success is more permanent when you achieve it without destroying your principles."

Walter Cronkite (1916 - 2009)

Television and radio broadcaster

5

"I long to accomplish a great and noble tasks, but it is my chief duty to accomplish humble tasks as though they were great and noble. The world is moved along, not only by the mighty shoves of its heroes, but also by the aggregate of the tiny pushes of each honest worker."

Helen Keller (1880 - 1968)

Author

6

"There are many aspects to success; material wealth is only one component. ...But success also includes good health, energy and enthusiasm for life, fulfilling relationships, creative freedom, emotional and psychological stability, a sense of well-being, and peace of mind."

Deepak Chopra (1946 -)

Alternative medicine advocate

7

"Success isn't everything but it makes a man stand straight."

Lillian Hellman (1905 - 1984)

Dramatist

8

"There is only one kind of success that really matters: the success of transforming ourselves, transforming our afflictions, fear, and anger. This is the kind of success, the kind of power, that will benefits us and others without causing any damage."

Thich Nhat Hanh (1926 -)

Monk

9

"Success is not greedy, as people think, but insignificant. That is why it satisfies nobody."

Lucius Annaeus Seneca (4 BC - 65 AD)

Philosopher

10

"There is always room at the top."

Daniel Webster (1782 - 1852)

Former United States Senator

11

"I'd rather attempt to do something great and fail than to attempt to do nothing and succeed."

Robert H. Schuller (1926 - 2015)

Televangelist

12

"Excess is success."

Roberto Cavalli (1940 -)

Founder of Roberto Cavalli

13

"The size of your success is measured by the strength of your desire; the size of your dream; and how you handle disappointment along the way."

Robert Kiyosaki (1947 -)

Businessman

14

"Success is doing ordinary things extraordinarily well."

Jim Rohn (1930 - 2009)

Entrepreneur

15

"Poor is the man whose pleasures depend on the permission of another."

Madonna (1958 -)

Singer-songwriter

16

"Success is liking yourself, liking what you do, and liking how you do it."

Maya Angelou (1928 - 2014)

Writer

17

"Success is not measured by what you accomplish, but by the opposition you have encountered, and the courage with which you have maintained the struggle against overwhelming odds."

Orison Swett Marden (1848 - 1924)

Author

18

"Success is survival."

Leonard Cohen (1934 - 2016)

Singer-songwriter

19

"If you want to be successful, just meditate, man. God will tell you what people need."

Carlos Santana (1947-)

Musician

20

"Success is finding, or making, that position which enables you to contribute to the world the very greatest services of which you are capable, through the diligent, persevering, resolute cultivation of all the faculties God has endowed you with, and doing it all with cheerfulness, scorning to allow difficulties or defeats to drive you to pessimism or despair. Success consists of being and doing, not simply accumulating. The businessman or business enterprise that aspires to win the highest recognition for success must distinguish himself or itself, not by the magnitude of the profits, but by the value of service performed."

B.C. Forbes (1880 - 1954)

Journalist

21

"Men are born to succeed-not to fail."

Henry David Thoreau (1817 - 1862)

Essayist

22

"Success is a lousy teacher. It seduces smart people into thinking they can't lose."

Bill Gates (1955 -)

Business magnate

23

"Possessions, outward success, publicity, luxury - to me these have always been contemptible. I believe that a simple and unassuming manner of life is best for everyone, best for both the body and the mind."

Albert Einstein (1879 - 1955)

Theoretical physicist

24

"Success consists of going from failure to failure without loss of enthusiasm."

Winston Churchill (1874 - 1965)

Former British Prime Minister

25

"Success is about enjoying what you have and where you are, while pursuing achievable goals."

Bo Bennett (1972 -)

Author

26

"Success is the sum of details."

Harvey S. Firestone (1868 - 1938)

Founder of Firestone Tire and Rubber Company

27

"A person is a success if they get up in the morning and gets to bed at night and in between does what he wants to do."

Bob Dylan (1941 -)

Singer-songwriter

28

"The measure of success is happiness and peace of mind."

Bobby Davro (1959 -)

Actor

29

"People don't need love. What they need is success in one form or another. It can be love but it needn't be."

Charles Bukowski (1920 - 1994)

Poet

30

"One fails forward toward success."

Charles Kettering (1876 - 1958)

Inventor

31

"Our greatest fear should not be of failure ... but of succeeding at things in life that don't really matter."

Francis Chan (1967-)

Pastor

32

"It's failure that gives you the proper perspective on success."

Ellen DeGeneres (1958-)

Comedian

33

"If you want total security, go to prison. There you're fed, clothed, given medical care and so on. The only thing lacking... is freedom."

Dwight D. Eisenhower (1890- 1969)

34th U. S. President

34

"The good news is that the moment you decide that what you know is more important than what you have been taught to believe, you will have shifted gears in your quest for abundance. Success comes from within, not from without."

Ralph Waldo Emerson (1803 - 1882)

Essayist

35

"Success is a poor teacher."

Robert Kiyosaki (1947 -)

Businessman

36

"Failure is success in progress."

Albert Einstein (1879 - 1955)

Theoretical physicist

37

"Never mind what others do; do better than yourself, beat your own record from day to day, and you are a success."

William J.H. Boetcker (1873 - 1962)

Motivational speaker

38

"The true success is the person who invented himself."

Al Goldstein (1936 - 2013)

Publisher

39

"Money won't create success, the freedom to make it will."

Nelson Mandela (1918 - 2013)

Activist

40

"The worst part of success is trying to find someone who is happy for you."

Bette Midler (1945-)

Singer

41

"Success is steady progress toward one's personal goals."

Jim Rohn (1930-2009)

Entrepreneur

42

"The greatest danger for most of us is not that our aim is too high and we miss it, but that it is too low and we reach it."

Michelangelo (1475-1564)

Sculptor

43

"Successful people are the ones who think up things for the rest of the world to keep busy at."

Don Marquis (1878 - 1937)

Humorist

44

"Try not to become a man of success. Rather become a man of value."

Albert Einstein (1879 - 1955)

Theoretical physicist

45

"Behind every successful person lies a pack of haters."

Eminem (1972 -)

Rapper

46

"Without continual growth and progress, such words as improvement, achievement, and success have no meaning."

Benjamin Franklin (1706 - 1790)

Founding Father of the United States

47

"The ladder of success is never crowded at the top."

Napoleon Hill (1883 - 1970)

Author

48

"Success comes from knowing that you did your best to become the best that you are capable of becoming."

John Wooden (1910 - 2010)

Basketball player

49

"There's a lot of blood, sweat, and guts between dreams and success."

Paul Bryant (1913 - 1983)

Football player

50

"I must admit that I personally measure success in terms of the contributions an individual makes to her or his fellow human beings."

Margaret Mead (1901 - 1978)

Anthropologist

51

"Being best is a false goal, you have to measure success on your own terms."

Damien Hirst (1965 -)

Artist

52

"Success is never final, failure is never fatal. It's courage that counts."

John Wooden (1910 - 2010)

Basketball player

53

"I'm a man, and I think every man wants to be No. 1."

Masayoshi Son (1957 -)

CEO of SoftBank

54

"I have learned that success is to be measured not so much by the position that one has reached in life as by the obstacles which he has overcome while trying to succeed."

Booker T. Washington (1856 - 1915)

Educator

55

"You know you are on the road to success if you would do your job, and not be paid for it."

Oprah Winfrey (1954 -)

Host of The Oprah Winfrey Show

56

"Success is not in what you have, but who you are."

Bo Bennett (1972 -)

Author

57

"Measure your success according to fun and creativity."

Anita Roddick (1942 - 2007)

Businesswoman

58

"Success is only meaningful and enjoyable if it feels like your own."

Michelle Obama (1964 -)

Former First Lady of the United States

59

"Each success only buys an admission ticket to a more difficult problem."

Henry A. Kissinger (1923 -)

Former United States Secretary of State

60

"Success is dependent on effort."

Sophocles (? - 406 BC)

Tragedian

61

"Success is a consequence and must not be a goal."

Gustave Flaubert (1821 - 1880)

Novelist

62

"Anyone whose goal is 'something higher' must expect someday to suffer vertigo. What is vertigo? Fear of falling? No, Vertigo is something other than fear of falling. It is the voice of the emptiness below us which tempts and lures us, it is the desire to fall, against which, terrified, we defend ourselves."

Milan Kundera (1929 -)

Writer

63

"Life is a succession of moments. To live each one is to succeed."

Corita Kent (1918 - 1986)

Artist

64

"Success unshared is failure."

John Paul DeJoria (1944 -)

Entrepreneur

65

"Anybody who's really successful has doubts."

Jerry Bruckheimer (1943 -)

Producer

66

"Success is like reaching an important birthday and finding you're exactly the same."

Audrey Hepburn (1929 - 1993)

Actress

67

"My mother drew a distinction between achievement and success. She said that achievement is the knowledge that you have studied and worked hard and done the best that is in you. Success is being praised by others, and that's nice, too, but not as important or satisfying. Always aim for achievement and forget about success."

Helen Hayes (1900 - 1993)

Actress

68

"Success is not a destination, but the road that you're on. Being successful means that you're working hard and walking your walk every day. You can only live your dream by working hard towards it. That's living your dream."

Marlon Wayans (1972 -)

Actor

69

"Judge your success by what you had to give up in order to get it."

Tenzin Gyatso (1935-)

14th Dalai Lama

70

"Success can't be forced."

Loretta Young (1913-2000)

Actress

71

"Success is not final, failure is not fatal: it is the courage to continue that counts."

Winston S. Churchill (1874-1965)

Former British Prime Minister

72

"I don't believe the most successful people are the ones who got the best grades, got into the best schools, or made the most money."

Ben Stein (1944 -)

Author

73

"Success in life is founded upon attention to the small things rather than to the large things; to the every day things nearest to us rather than to the things that are remote and uncommon."

Booker T. Washington (1856 - 1915)

Educator

74

"Success is stumbling from failure to failure with no loss of enthusiasm."

Winston S. Churchill (1874 - 1965)

Former British Prime Minister

75

"To me success means effectiveness in the world, that I am able to carry my ideas and values into the world – that I am able to change it in positive ways."

Maxine Hong Kingston (1940 -)

Author

76

"Success is a state of mind. If you want success, start thinking of yourself as a success."

Joyce Brothers (1927 - 2013)

Psychologist

77

"If you set your goals ridiculously high and it's a failure, you will fail above everyone else's success."

James Cameron (1954 -)

Filmmaker

78

"I do not like to repeat successes. I like to go on to other things."

Walt Disney (1901 - 1966)

Entrepreneur

79

"Success is a lot like a bright, white tuxedo. You feel terrific when you get it, but then you're desperately afraid of getting it dirty, of spoiling it in any way."

Conan O'Brien (1963 -)

Television host

80

"Those who succeed and are happy know that the goal is to be authentic and memorable and make a difference, not to be understood and liked by everyone."

Neil Strauss (1969 -)

Writer

81

"What is success? I think it is a mixture of having a flair for the thing that you are doing; knowing that it is not enough, that you have got to have hard work and a certain sense of purpose."

Margaret Thatcher (1925 - 2013)

Former British Prime Minister

82

"Those who try to do something and fail are infinitely better than those who try nothing and succeed."

Lloyd Jones (1955 -)

Author

83

"Success is to be measured not so much by the position that one has reached in life as by the obstacles which he has overcome."

Booker T. Washington (1856 - 1915)

Educator

84

"Success is the fruit of concentration."

Navjot Singh Sidhu (1963 -)

Politician

85

"If I tell you I'm good, probably you will say I'm boasting. But if I tell you I'm not good, you'll know I'm lying."

Bruce Lee (1940 - 1973)

Martial artist

86

"The whole secret of a successful life is to find out what is one's destiny to do, and then do it."

Henry Ford (1863 - 1947)

Founder of Ford Motor Company

87

"If you have no critics you'll likely have no success."

Malcolm X (1925 - 1965)

Minister

88

"My mother said to me, "If you become a soldier, you'll be a general; if you become a monk, you'll end up as the Pope." Instead, I became a painter and wound up as Picasso."

Pablo Picasso (1881 - 1973)

Painter

89

"If you're in the luckiest one per cent of humanity, you owe it to the rest of humanity to think about the other 99 per cent."

Warren Buffett (1930 -)

Investor

90

"There's a ball. There's a hoop. You put the ball through the hoop. That's success."

Kareem Abdul-Jabbar (1947-)

Basketball player

91

**"Success is...
knowing your purpose in life,
growing to reach your maximum potential, and
sowing seeds that benefit others."**

John C. Maxwell (1947-)

Author

92

"Success means doing the best we can with what we have. Success is the doing, not the getting; in the trying, not the triumph. Success is a personal standard, reaching for the highest that is in us, becoming all that we can be."

Zig Ziglar (1926 - 2012)

Salesman

93

"Success is...knowing your purpose in life, growing to reach your maximum potential, and sowing seeds that benefit others."

John C. Maxwell (1947-)

Author

94

"Eighty percent of success is showing up."

Woody Allen (1935-)

Director

95

"Success is the progressive realization of a worthy goal or ideal."

Earl Nightingale (1921- 1989)

Author

96

"True success, true happiness lies in freedom and fulfillment."

Dada Vaswani (1918 -)

Indian spiritual leader

97

"Success means having the courage, the determination, and the will to become the person you believe you were meant to be."

George Sheehan (1918 - 1993)

Physician

98

"Success means we go to sleep at night knowing that our talents and ablities were used in a way that served others."

Marianne Williamson (1952 -)

Inspirational Author and Speaker

99

"A man is a success if he gets up in the morning and gets to bed at night, and in between he does what he wants to do."

Bob Dylan (1941-)

Singer-songwriter

100

"No matter how successful you are in your career, you must always remember that we are here to live. If you keep yourself busy working, you will surely regret it."

Jack Ma (1964-)

Founder and Executive Chairman of Alibaba Group

101

"Success is not to be pursued; it is to be attracted by the person you become."

Jim Rohn (1930 - 2009)

Entrepreneur

102

"You are not here merely to make a living. You are here in order to enable the world to live more amply, with greater vision, with a finer spirit of hope and achievement. You are here to enrich the world, and you impoverish yourself if you forget the errand."

Woodrow Wilson (1856 - 1924)

28th U. S. President

103

"Success is getting what you want, happiness is wanting what you get"

W. P. Kinsella (1935 - 2016)

Author

104

"The reward for work well done is the opportunity to do more."

Jonas Salk (1914 - 1995)

Medical researcher

105

"Success is full of promise till one gets it, and then it seems like a nest from which the bird has flown."

Henry Ward Beecher (1813 - 1887)

Protestant Clergyman

106

"If I cannot do great things, I can do small things in a great way."

Martin Luther King Jr. (1929 - 1968)

Minister

107

"Success is never final, but failure can be."

Bill Parcells (1941 -)

Football coach

108

"Success is most often achieved by those who don't know that failure is inevitable."

Coco Chanel (1883 - 1971)

Milliner

109

"Success is not forever and failure isn't fatal."

Don Shula (1930 -)

Football player

110

"A successful man is one who makes more money than his wife can spend. A successful woman is one who can find such a man."

Lana Turner (1921 - 1995)

Actress

111

"I have had all of the disadvantages required for success."

Larry Ellison (1944 -)

Executive Chairman and CTO of Oracle Corporation

112

"What material success does is provide you with the ability to concentrate on other things that really matter. And that is being able to make a difference, not only in your own life, but in other people's lives."

Oprah Winfrey (1954 -)

Host of The Oprah Winfrey Show

113

"Nothing succeeds like success."

Alexandre Dumas (1802 - 1870)

Novelist

114

"Success is the sweetest revenge."

Vanessa Williams (1963 -)

Actress

115

"Sometimes it takes a good fall to really know where you stand"

Hayley Williams (1988 -)

Singer

116

"Conquer, but don't triumph."

Marie Von Ebner-Eschenbach (1830 - 1916)

Novelist

117

"Success is like winning the sweepstakes or getting killed in an automobile crash. It always happens to somebody else."

Allan Sherman (1924 - 1973)

Comedy writer

118

"The test of success is not what you do when you are on top. Success is how high you bounce when you hit the bottom."

George S. Patton Jr. (1885 - 1945)

Senior officer

119

"It is better to fail in originality than to succeed in imitation."

Herman Melville (1819 - 1891)

Novelist

120

**"Success is getting what you want..
Happiness is wanting what you get."**

Dale Carnegie (1888 - 1955)

Writer

121

**"The distance between insanity and genius is
measured only by success."**

Bruce Feirstein (1956 -)

Screenwriter

122

**"True success is the only thing that you cannot have
unless and until you have offered it to others."**

Sri Chinmoy (1931 - 2007)

Spiritual teacher

123

"Success is never accidental."

Jack Dorsey (1976 -)

CEO of Twitter Inc.

124

"Our greatest fear should not be of failure but of succeeding at things in life that don't really matter."

Francis Chan (1967 -)

Pastor

125

"To laugh often and much; to win the respect of intelligent people and the affection of children... to leave the world a better place... to know even one life has breathed easier because you have lived. This is to have succeeded."

Ralph Waldo Emerson (1803 - 1882)

Essayist

126

"To follow without halt, one aim; there is the secret of success. And success? What is it? I do not find it in the applause of the theater; it lies rather in the satisfaction of accomplishment."

Anna Pavlova (1881 - 1931)

Ballerina

127

"He has achieved success who has worked well, laughed often, and loved much."

Elbert Hubbard (1856 - 1915)

Writer

128

"It is a mistake to suppose that men succeed through success; they much oftener succeed through failures. Precept, study, advice, and example could never have taught them so well as failure has done."

Samuel Smiles (1812 - 1904)

Author

129

"Our best successes often come after our greatest disappointments."

Henry Ward Beecher (1813 - 1887)

Protestant Clergyman

130

"Success is how high you bounce when you hit bottom."

George S. Patton (1885 - 1945)

Senior officer

131

"I wanted to be successful, not famous."

George Harrison (1943 - 2001)

Guitarist

132

"To be great is to be misunderstood."

Ralph Waldo Emerson (1803 - 1882)

Essayist

133

"A thinker sees his own actions as experiments and questions – as attempts to find out something. Success and failure are for him answers above all."

Friedrich Nietzsche (1844 - 1900)

Philosopher

134

"We are all failures- at least the best of us are."

J.M. Barrie (1860 - 1937)

Novelist

135

"Success – keeping your mind awake and your desire asleep."

Walter Scott (1771 - 1832)

Historical novelist

136

"Sometimes I worry about being a success in a mediocre world."

Lily Tomlin (1939 -)

Actress

137

"Success is a journey, not a destination. The doing is often more important than the outcome."

Arthur Ashe (1943 - 1993)

Tennis player

138

"I honestly think it is better to be a failure at something you love than to be a success at something you hate."

George Burns (1896 - 1996)

Actor

139

"So I feel like success is opportunity plus preparation, so work begets work, and as long as you're prepared it's going to continue to come your way."

Anthony Mackie (1978 -)

Actor

140

"I measure success in terms of the contributions an individual makes to her fellow human beings."

Margaret Mead (1901 - 1978)

Anthropologist

141

"Success is when the checks don't bounce."

Andy Warhol (1928 - 1987)

Artist

142

"Success is the child of audacity."

Benjamin Disraeli (1804 - 1881)

Former British Prime Minister

143

"Good people are good because they've come to wisdom through failure. We get very little wisdom from success, you know."

William Saroyan (1908 - 1981)

Novelist

144

"Success is focusing the full power of all you are on what you have a burning desire to achieve."

Wilfred Peterson (1900 - 1995)

Author

145

"Nothing fails like success."

Alan Watts (1915 - 1973)

Philosopher

146

"Success is 1% inspiration, 99% perspiration."

Thomas A. Edison (1847 - 1931)

Inventor

147

"It is on our failures that we base a new and different and better success."

Havelock Ellis (1859 - 1939)

Physician

148

"Fame and success are very different things."

Enya (1961-)

Singer

149

"Try not to become a man of success, but a man of value. Look around at how people want to get more out of life than they put in. A man of value will give more than he receives. Be creative, but make sure that what you create is not a curse for mankind."

Albert Einstein (1879 - 1955)

Theoretical physicist

150

"When it comes to success, there are no shortcuts."

Bo Bennett (1972 -)

Author

151

"Success is the progressive realization of predetermined, worthwhile, personal goals."

Paul J. Meyer (1928 - 2009)

Author

SUCCESS: *How to Get it?*

152

"Sooner or later, those who win are those who think they can."

Richard Bach (1936 -)

Writer

153

"Ability is nothing without opportunity."

Napoleon Bonaparte (1769 - 1821)

Statesman

154

"Start by doing what's necessary; then do what's possible; and suddenly you are doing the impossible."

Francis of Assisi (1181 - 1226)

Saint

155

"I have learnt to be even more patient."

Roger Federer (1981 -)

Tennis player

156

"We all naturally want to become successful... we also want to take shortcuts. And it's easy to do so, but you can never take away the effort of hard work and discipline and sacrifice."

Apolo Ohno (1982 -)

Short track speed skater

157

"I advise you to stop sharing your dreams with people who try to hold you back, even if they're your parents. Because, if you're the kind of person who senses there's something out there for you beyond whatever it is you're expected to do - if you want to be EXTRA-ordinary- you will not get there by hanging around a bunch of people who tell you you're not extraordinary. Instead, you will probably become as ordinary as they expect you to be."

Kelly Cutrone (1965-)

Publicist

158

"Set your goals high, and don't stop till you get there."

Bo Jackson (1962-)

Football player

159

"I am a slow walker, but I never walk back."

Abraham Lincoln (1809 - 1865)

16th U. S. President

160

"The person who makes a success of living is the one who sees his goal steadily and aims for it unswervingly."

Cecil B. DeMille (1881 - 1959)

Producer

161

"If A is a success in life, then A equals x plus y plus z. Work is x; y is play; and z is keeping your mouth shut."

Albert Einstein (1879 - 1955)

Theoretical physicist

162

"You have to make it happen."

Denis Diderot (1713 - 1784)

Philosopher

163

"Do your duty and a little more and the future will take care of itself."

Andrew Carnegie (1835 - 1919)

Industrialist

164

"I never dreamed about success, I worked for it."

Estee Lauder (1908 - 2004)

Businessperson

165

"Perseverance is not a long race; it is many short races one after the other."

Walter Elliot (1888 - 1958)

Politician

166

"Yesterday I dared to struggle. Today I dare to win."

Bernadette Devlin (1947 -)

Politician

167

"Kites rise highest against the wind, not with it."

Winston S. Churchill (1874 - 1965)

Former British Prime Minister

168

"Success is achieved by developing our strengths, not by eliminating our weaknesses."

Marilyn vos Savant (1946 -)

Author

169

"Would you like me to give you a formula for success? It's quite simple, really: Double your rate of failure. You are thinking of failure as the enemy of success. But it isn't at all. You can be discouraged by failure or you can learn from it, so go ahead and make mistakes. Make all you can. Because remember that's where you will find success."

Thomas J. Watson (1874 - 1956)

Chairman and CEO of IBM

170

"Success usually comes to those who are too busy to be looking for it."

Henry David Thoreau (1817 - 1862)

Essayist

171

"I can't give you a sure-fire formula for success, but I can give you a formula for failure: try to please everybody all the time."

Herbert Bayard Swope (1882 - 1958)

Editor

172

"The successful people of this world take life as it comes. They just go out and deal with the world as it is."

Ben Stein (1944 -)

Author

173

"Don't spend time beating on a wall, hoping to transform it into a door."

Coco Chanel (1883 - 1971)

Milliner

174

"Don't think, just do."

Horace (65 BC - 8 BC)

Poet

175

"Fear of failure, it's the greatest motivational tool. It drives me and drives me and drives me."

Jerry West (1938 -)

Basketball player

176

"Through perseverance many people win success out of what seemed destined to be certain failure."

Benjamin Disraeli (1804 - 1881)

Former British Prime Minister

177

"The secret of success is sincerity."

Jean Giraudoux (1882 - 1944)

Dramatist

178

"If at first you don't succeed, destroy all evidence that you tried."

Steven Wright (1955 -)

Stand-up comedian

179

"People rarely succeed unless they have fun in what they are doing."

Dale Carnegie (1888 - 1955)

Writer

180

"Integrity is the essence of everything successful."

R. Buckminster Fuller (1895 - 1983)

Designer

181

"Motivation will almost always beat mere talent."

Norman Ralph Augustine (1935 -)

Chairman of the Review of United States Human Space Flight Plans Committee

182

"A will finds a way."

Orison Swett Marden (1848 - 1924)

Author

183

"Life is a journey. When we stop, things don't go right."

Pope Francis (1936 -)

266th and current Pope

184

"All you need in this life is ignorance and confidence; then success is sure."

Mark Twain (1835 - 1910)

Writer

185

"I am not a has-been. I am a will be."

Lauren Bacall (1924 - 2014)

Actress

186

"Whosoever desires constant success must change his conduct with the times."

Niccolò Machiavelli (1469 - 1527)

Diplomat

187

"Always bear in mind that your own resolution to succeed is more important than any one thing."

Abraham Lincoln (1809 - 1865)

16th U. S. President

188

"Don't mistake activity with achievement."

John Wooden (1910 - 2010)

Basketball player

189

"Don't watch the clock; do what it does. Keep going."

Sam Levenson (1911 - 1980)

Humorist

190

"I don't believe you have to be better than everybody else. I believe you have to be better than you ever thought you could be."

Ken Venturi (1931 - 2013)

Golfer

191

"Either get busy living or get busy dying."

Stephen King (1947 -)

Writer

192

"If you believe you can, you might. If you know you can, you will."

Steve Maraboli (1975 -)

Researcher

193

"Success is almost totally dependent upon drive and persistence. The extra energy required to make another effort or try another approach is the secret of winning."

Denis Waitley (1933 -)

Motivational speaker

194

"You cannot dream yourself into a character; you must hammer and forge yourself one."

James A. Froude (1818 - 1894)

Historian

195

"The secret to success is to know something nobody else knows."

Aristotle Onassis (1906 - 1975)

Shipping tycoon

196

"Life is like riding a bicycle. To keep your balance you must keep moving."

Albert Einstein (1879 - 1955)

Theoretical physicist

197

"You aren't going to find anybody that's going to be successful without making a sacrifice and without perseverance."

Lou Holtz (1937 -)

Football player

198

"Don't wait. The time will never be just right."

Napoleon Hill (1883 - 1970)

Author

199

"Go as far as you can see; when you get there, you'll be able to see farther."

J. P. Morgan (1837 - 1913)

Financier

200

"Aim for the moon. If you miss, you may hit a star."

W. Clement Stone (1902 - 2002)

Businessman

201

"Don't count the days, make the days count."

Muhammad Ali (1942 - 2016)

Boxer

202

"How do you know you're going to do something, untill you do it?"

J. D. Salinger (1919 - 2010)

Writer

203

"I can't imagine a person becoming a success who doesn't give this game of life everything he's got."

Walter Cronkite (1916 - 2009)

Television and radio broadcaster

204

"The will to win, the desire to succeed, the urge to reach your full potential... these are the keys that will unlock the door to personal excellence."

Confucius (551 BC - 479 BC)

Chinese teacher

205

"The ladder of success is best climbed by stepping on the rungs of opportunity."

Ayn Rand (1905 - 1982)

Writer

206

"When you take risks you learn that there will be times when you succeed and there will be times when you fail, and both are equally important."

Ellen DeGeneres (1958 -)

Comedian

207

"Learn from the past, set vivid, detailed goals for the future, and live in the only moment of time over which you have any control: now."

Denis Waitley (1933 -)

Motivational speaker

208

"The public has an appetite for anything about imagination - anything that is as far away from reality as is creatively possible."

Steven Spielberg (1946 -)

Filmmaker

209

"The moment we believe that success is determined by an ingrained level of ability as opposed to resilience and hard work, we will be brittle in the face of adversity."

Joshua Waitzkin (1976 -)

Chess player

210

"Move fast and break things. Unless you are breaking stuff, you are not moving fast enough."

Mark Zuckerberg (1984 -)

CEO of Facebook

211

"I've worked too hard and too long to let anything stand in the way of my goals. I will not let my teammates down and I will not let myself down."

Mia Hamm (1972-)

Soccer player

212

"To know oneself, one should assert oneself."

Albert Camus (1913- 1960)

Philosopher

213

"Success has a simple formula: do your best, and people may like it."

Sam Ewing (1949-)

Baseball player

214

"We are taught you must blame your father, your sisters, your brothers, the school, the teachers - but never blame yourself. It's never your fault. But it's always your fault, because if you wanted to change you're the one who has got to change."

Katharine Hepburn (1907 - 2003)

Actress

215

"The key is over time. Success is built sequentially. It's one thing at a time."

Gary Keller (1944 -)

Entrepreneur

216

"In order to succeed, your desire for success should be greater than your fear of failure."

Bill Cosby (1937 -)

Actor

217

"I've come to believe that each of us has a personal calling that's as unique as a fingerprint - and that the best way to succeed is to discover what you love and then find a way to offer it to others in the form of service, working hard, and also allowing the energy of the universe to lead you."

Oprah Winfrey (1954-)

Host of The Oprah Winfrey Show

218

"It's fine to celebrate success but it is more important to heed the lessons of failure."

Bill Gates (1955-)

Business magnate

219

"Dictionary is the only place that success comes before work. Hard work is the price we must pay for success. I think you can accomplish anything if you're willing to pay the price."

Vince Lombardi (1913 - 1970)

Football player

220

"Change your life today. Don't gamble on the future, act now, without delay."

Simone de Beauvoir (1908 - 1986)

Writer

221

"Success is a little like wrestling a gorilla. You don't quit when you're tired. You quit when the gorilla is tired."

Robert Strauss (1913 - 1975)

Actor

222

"I owe my success to having listened respectfully to the very best advice, and then going away and doing the exact opposite."

G. K. Chesterton (1874 - 1936)

Journalist

223

"Only I can change my life. No one can do it for me."

Carol Burnett (1933 -)

Actress

224

"If at first you don't succeed, try, try again. Then quit. No use being a damn fool about it."

W.C. Fields (1880 - 1946)

Actor

225

"Do the one thing you think you cannot do. Fail at it. Try again. Do better the second time. The only people who never tumble are those who never mount the high wire. This is your moment. Own it."

Oprah Winfrey (1954 -)

Host of The Oprah Winfrey Show

226

"The way of success is the way of continuous pursuit of knowledge."

Napoleon Hill (1883 - 1970)

Author

227

"All successful people men and women are big dreamers. They imagine what their future could be, ideal in every respect, and then they work every day toward their distant vision, that goal or purpose."

Brian Tracy (1944 -)

Motivational speaker

228

"If you want to increase your success rate, double your failure rate."

Thomas J. Watson (1874 - 1956)

Chairman and CEO of IBM

229

"Love yourself first and everything else falls into line. You really have to love yourself to get anything done in this world."

Lucille Ball (1911 - 1989)

Actress

230

"I learned to always take on things I'd never done before. Growth and comfort do not coexist."

Virginia Rometty (1957 -)

Chairman

231

"Many are called but few get up."

Oliver Herford (1863 - 1935)

Illustrator

232

"Do the difficult things while they are easy and do the great things while they are small. A journey of a thousand miles must begin with a single step."

Lao Tzu (? - 533 BC)

Chinese philosopher

233

"It had long since come to my attention that people of accomplishment rarely sat back and let things happen to them. They went out and happened to things."

Leonardo da Vinci (1452 - 1519)

Polymath

234

"Six essential qualities that are the key to success: Sincerity, personal integrity, humility, courtesy, wisdom, charity."

William Menninger (1899 - 1966)

Psychiatrist

235

"The key to my success has been to give up everything for my dream."

John H. Johnson (1918 - 2005)

Businessman

236

"What you do today can improve all your tomorrows."

Ralph Marston (1907 -)

Football player

237

"You can't cross the sea merely by standing and staring at the water."

Rabindranath Tagore (1861 - 1941)

Writer

238

"Leap, and the net will appear."

John Burroughs (1837 -)

Essayist

239

"Expect problems and eat them for breakfast."

Alfred A. Montapert (1906 - 1997)

Author

240

"The path to success is to take massive, determined action."

Tony Robbins (1960 -)

Entrepreneur

241

"90% of your plans are going to fail no matter what you do. Get used to it."

Mark Manson (1984 -)

Writer

242

"Keep on going, and the chances are that you will stumble on something, perhaps when you are least expecting it. I never heard of anyone ever stumbling on something sitting down."

Charles F. Kettering (1876 - 1958)

Inventor

243

"Take time to deliberate; but when the time for action arrives, stop thinking and go in."

Napoleon Bonaparte (1769 - 1821)

Statesman

244

"Why be a king, when you can be a god?"

Eminem (1972 -)

Rapper

245

"One way to keep momentum going is to have constantly greater goals."

Michael Korda (1933 -)

Writer

246

"Do not be embarrassed by your failures, learn from them and start again."

Richard Branson (1950 -)

Business magnate

247

"The most successful men in the end are those whose success is the result of steady accretion."

Alexander Graham Bell (1847 - 1922)

Engineer

248

"If you're offered a seat on a rocket ship, don't ask what seat! Just get on."

Sheryl Sandberg (1969 -)

COO of Facebook

249

"Every man has a right to be conceited until he is successful."

Benjamin Disraeli (1804 - 1881)

Former British Prime Minister

250

"Most of the successful people I've known are the ones who do more listening than talking."

Bernard Baruch (1870 - 1965)

Financier

251

"Stop chasing the money and start chasing the passion."

Tony Hsieh (1973 -)

CEO of Zappos

252

"The secret to success is to offend the greatest number of people."

George Bernard Shaw (1856 - 1950)

Playwright

253

"Success is achieved and maintained by those who try and keep trying."

W. Clement Stone (1902 - 2002)

Businessman

254

"Great achievers are driven, not so much by the pursuit of success, but by the fear of failure."

Larry Ellison (1944 -)

Executive Chairman and CTO of Oracle Corporation

255

"Nothing in the world can take the place of perseverance. Talent will not; nothing is more common than unsuccessful people with talent. Genius will not; unrewarded genius is almost legendary. Education will not; the world is full of educated derelicts. Perseverance and determination alone are omnipotent."

Calvin Coolidge (1872 - 1933)

30th U. S. President

256

"I have been insane on the subject of moneymaking all my life."

Cornelius Vanderbilt (1794 - 1877)

Business magnate

257

"The real test is not whether you avoid this failure, because you won't. It's whether you let it harden or shame you into inaction, or whether you learn from it; whether you choose to persevere."

Barack Obama (1961-)

44th U. S. President

258

"We need to internalize this idea of excellence. Not many folks spend a lot of time trying to be excellent."

Barack Obama (1961-)

44th U. S. President

259

"Successful people do what unsuccessful people are not willing to do. Don't wish it were easier; wish you were better."

Jim Rohn (1930 - 2009)

Entrepreneur

260

"One thing I've learned over the years from my core set, the LAST ONE (set) is the most important one. Because THAT'S WHEN you start improving. THAT'S WHEN the work pays off now. Because your legs are DEAD and you gotta push your body. It's like moving past a barrier."

Usain Bolt (1986 -)

Olympic athlete

261

"Being a part of success is more important than being personally indispensable."

Pat Riley (1945-)

President of the Miami Heat

262

"You never achieve success unless you like what you are doing."

Dale Carnegie (1888 - 1955)

Writer

263

"Do your work with your whole heart, and you will succeed - there's so little competition."

Elbert Hubbard (1856 - 1915)

Writer

264

"Your true success in life begins only when you make the commitment to become excellent at what you do."

Brian Tracy (1944 -)

Motivational speaker

265

"The key to success? Work hard, stay focused and marry a Kennedy."

Arnold Schwarzenegger (1947 -)

Former Governor of California

266

"Who seeks shall find."

Sophocles (? - 406 BC)

Tragedian

267

"People who are unable to motivate themselves must be content with mediocrity, no matter how impressive their other talents."

Andrew Carnegie (1835 - 1919)

Industrialist

268

"Combining all of those skills together, the art and the science, the thinking and the doing, was what resulted in the exceptional result."

Steve Jobs (1955 - 2011)

Co-founder, Chairman, and CEO of Apple Inc.

269

"Act as if what you do makes a difference. It does."

William James (1842 - 1910)

Philosopher

270

"To be a good loser is to learn how to win."

Carl Sandburg (1878 - 1967)

Journalist

271

"All you need is ignorance and confidence and the success is sure."

Mark Twain (1835 - 1910)

Writer

272

"A strong, successful man is not the victim of his environment. He creates favorable conditions. His own inherent force and energy compel things to turn out as he desires."

Orison Swett Marden (1848 - 1924)

Author

273

"Ambition is the path to success. Persistence is the vehicle you arrive in."

Bill Bradley (1943 -)

American senator

274

"You're not obligated to win. You're obligated to keep trying. Do the best you can do everyday."

Jason Mraz (1977 -)

Singer-songwriter

275

"Striving for success without hard work is like trying to harvest where you haven't planted."

David Bly (1952 -)

Politician

276

"The more things you do, the more you can do."

Lucille Ball (1911 - 1989)

Actress

277

"If you ask me what I came into this life to do, I will tell you: I came to live out loud."

Emile Zola (1840 - 1902)

Novelist

278

"The will to succeed is important, but what's more important is the will to prepare."

Bobby Knight (1940 -)

Basketball coach

279

"Accept the challenges so that you can feel the exhilaration of victory."

George S. Patton (1885 - 1945)

Senior officer

280

"Aim for success, not perfection. Never give up your right to be wrong, because then you will lose the ability to learn new things and move forward with your life. Remember that fear always lurks behind perfectionism."

David M. Burns (1942 -)

Author

281

"Go for it now. The future is promised to no one."

Wayne Dyer (1940 - 2015)

Teacher

282

"A clear vision, backed by definite plans, gives you a tremendous feeling of confidence and personal power."

Brian Tracy (1944 -)

Motivational speaker

283

"Reputation is the key to success. You have to be loyal to your customers."

Li Ka Shing (1928 -)

Chairman of Li Ka Shing Foundation

284

"Even if you fall on your face, you're still moving forward."

Victor Kiam (1926 - 2001)

Chairman

285

"Nobody got anywhere in the world by simply being content."

Louis L'Amour (1908 - 1988)

Novelist

286

"Success doesn't come to you, you've got to go to it."

Marva Collins (1936 - 2015)

Educator

287

"You don't learn to walk by following rules. You learn by doing, and by falling over."

Richard Branson (1950 -)

Business magnate

288

"You have to set yourself goals so you can push yourself harder. Desire is the key to success."

Usain Bolt (1986 -)

Olympic athlete

289

"On the clarity of your ideas depends the scope of your success in any endeavor."

James Robertson (1958 -)

Writer

290

"If everyone is moving forward together, then success takes care of itself."

Henry Ford (1863 - 1947)

Founder of Ford Motor Company

291

"Train yourself to let go of the things you fear to lose."

George Lucas (1944 -)

Filmmaker

292

"Don't let what you cannot do interfere with what you can do."

John Wooden (1910 - 2010)

Basketball player

293

"There is little success where there is little laughter."

Andrew Carnegie (1835 - 1919)

Industrialist

294

"You will never win if you never begin."

Helen Rowland (1875 - 1950)

Journalist

295

"Success comes from curiosity, concentration, perseverance and self-criticism."

Albert Einstein (1879 - 1955)

Theoretical physicist

296

"All our dreams can come true if we have the courage to pursue them."

Walt Disney (1901 - 1966)

Entrepreneur

297

"The secret of success is to do the common thing uncommonly well."

John D. Rockefeller Jr. (1874 - 1960)

Financier

298

"Quality is not an act, it is a habit."

Aristotle (384 BC - 322 BC)

Philosopher

299

"Success comes when people act together; failure tends to happen alone."

Deepak Chopra (1946 -)

Alternative medicine advocate

300

"To fly, we have to have resistance."

Maya Lin (1959 -)

Designer

301

"I haven't invented anything earth-shattering. If I could be said to have one noteworthy ability compared with the average person, it's that I have a keen interest in reading the direction and timing of paradigm shifts."

Masayoshi Son (1957 -)

CEO of SoftBank

302

"You can design and create, and build the most wonderful place in the world. But it takes people to make the dream a reality."

Walt Disney (1901 - 1966)

Entrepreneur

303

"Experience shows that success is due less to ability than to zeal."

Charles Buxton (1823 - 1871)

Brewer

304

"A constant struggle, a ceaseless battle to bring success from inhospitable surroundings, is the price of all great achievements."

Orison Swett Marden (1848 - 1924)

Author

305

"The only place where success comes before work is in the dictionary."

Vidal Sassoon (1928 - 2012)

Hair stylist

306

"I have always served the public to the best of my ability. Why? Because, like every other man, it is to my interest to do so."

Cornelius Vanderbilt (1794 - 1877)

Business magnate

307

"Letting go means to come to the realization that some people are a part of your history, but not a part of your destiny."

Steve Maraboli (1975 -)

Researcher

308

"The dog that trots about finds a bone."

Golda Meir (1898 - 1978)

Former Prime Minister of Israel

309

"Well done is better than well said."

Benjamin Franklin (1706 - 1790)

Founding Father of the United States

310

"Coming together is a beginning. Keeping together is progress. Working together is success."

Henry Ford (1863 - 1947)

Founder of Ford Motor Company

311

"Anyone can be a millionaire, but to become a billionaire you need an astrologer."

J. P. Morgan (1837 - 1913)

Financier

312

"Patience, persistence and perspiration make an unbeatable combination for success."

Napoleon Hill (1883 - 1970)

Author

313

"There is progress whether ye are going forward or backward! The thing is to move!"

Edgar Cayce (1877 - 1945)

Mystic

314

"I was smart enough to go through any door that opened."

Joan Rivers (1933 - 2014)

Stand-up comedian

315

"Get action. Seize the moment. Man was never intended to become an oyster."

Theodore Roosevelt (1858 - 1919)

26th U. S. President

316

"No bird soars too high if he soars with his own wings."

William Blake (1757 - 1827)

Poet

317

"Deserve your dream."

Octavio Paz (1914 - 1998)

Writer

318

"Believe in yourself! Have faith in your abilities! Without a humble but reasonable confidence in your own powers you cannot be successful or happy."

Norman Vincent Peale (1898 - 1993)

Minister

319

"You simply have to put one foot in front of the other and keep going. Put blinders on and plow right ahead."

George Lucas (1944 -)

Filmmaker

320

"Celebrate what you've accomplished, but raise the bar a little higher each time you succeed."

Mia Hamm (1972-)

Soccer player

321

"It is very important to know who you are. To make decisions. To show who you are."

Malala Yousafzai (1997-)

Activist for female education

322

"Life is 10% what happens to you and 90% how you react to it."

Charles R. Swindoll (1934-)

Pastor

323

"The ability to convert ideas to things is the secret of outward success."

Henry Ward Beecher (1813 - 1887)

Protestant Clergyman

324

"Don't let the fear of striking out hold you back."

Babe Ruth (1895 -)

Baseball player

325

"I don't work for the others, I work for myself. And I chose the way to work for myself. But working for myself, that means working for the society. If you really want to work for yourself, think about the others, the DT time, making sure you help others, because only when the other people are successful, when the other people are happy, you'll be successful, you'll be happy."

Jack Ma (1964 -)

Founder and Executive Chairman of Alibaba Group

326

"Victory belongs to the most persevering."

Napoleon Bonaparte (1769 - 1821)

Statesman

327

"The person who tries to live alone will not succeed as a human being. His heart withers if it does not answer another heart. His mind shrinks away if he hears only the echoes of his own thoughts and finds no other inspiration."

Pearl S. Buck (1892 - 1973)

Writer

328

"I am not a product of my circumstances. I am a product of my decisions."

Stephen Covey (1932 - 2012)

Educator

329

"Success isn't always about 'Greatness', it's about consistency. Consistent, hard work gains success. Greatness will come."

Dwayne Johnson (1972 -)

Actor

330

"Ever tried. Ever failed. No matter. Try Again. Fail again. Fail better."

Samuel Beckett (1906 - 1989)

Novelist

331

"I attribute my success to this - I never gave or took any excuse."

Florence Nightingale (1820 - 1910)

Statistician

332

"Success does not consist in never making mistakes but in never making the same one a second time."

George Bernard Shaw (1856 - 1950)

Playwright

333

"Everyone has a plan until they get punched in the mouth."

Mike Tyson (1966 -)

Boxer

334

"Successful people are always looking for opportunities to help others. Unsuccessful people are always asking, "What's in it for me?"

Brian Tracy (1944 -)

Motivational speaker

335

"There are better starters than me but I'm a strong finisher."

Usain Bolt (1986 -)

Olympic athlete

336

"You can't build a reputation on what you are going to do."

Henry Ford (1863 - 1947)

Founder of Ford Motor Company

337

"People who succeed have momentum. The more they succeed, the more they want to succeed, and the more they find a way to succeed. Similarly, when someone is failing, the tendency is to get on a downward spiral that can even become a self-fulfilling prophecy."

Tony Robbins (1960 -)

Entrepreneur

338

"When you expect things to happen - strangely enough - they do happen."

J. P. Morgan (1837 - 1913)

Financier

339

"I'm not one of those people who thinks they simply deserve success. I have the drive to work."

Bridget Moynahan (1971 -)

Actress

340

"Opportunity does not knock, it presents itself when you beat down the door."

Kyle Chandler (1965 -)

Actor

341

"You've got to get up every morning with determination if you're going to go to bed with satisfaction."

George Lorimer (1867 - 1937)

Journalist

342

"The season of failure is the best time for sowing the seeds of success."

Paramahansa Yogananda (1893 - 1952)

Guru

343

"God always strives together with those who strive."

Aeschylus (? - ?)

Tragedian

344

"Before anything else, preparation is the key to success."

Alexander Graham Bell (1847 - 1922)

Engineer

345

"You sort of start thinking anything's possible if you've got enough nerve."

J. K. Rowling (1965 -)

Novelist

346

"You will never find time for anything. If you want time you must make it."

Charles Buxton (1823 - 1871)

Brewer

347

"When the water starts boiling it is foolish to turn off the heat."

Nelson Mandela (1918 - 2013)

Activist

348

"You do not succeed because you do not know what you want, or you don't want it intensely enough."

Frank Crane (1861 - 1928)

Presbyterian minister

349

"I don't dwell on success. Maybe that's one reason I'm successful."

Calvin Klein (1968 -)

Fashion designer

350

"I'm convinced that about half of what separates successful entrepreneurs from the non successful entrepreneurs is pure perseverance. It is so hard, you pour so much of your life into this thing, there are such rough moments in time, that most people give up. I don't blame them, it's really tough."

Steve Jobs (1955 - 2011)

Co-founder, Chairman, and CEO of Apple Inc.

351

"No matter how many goals you have achieved, you must set your sights on a higher one."

Jessica Savitch (1947 - 1983)

Television journalist

352

"Success in life comes not from holding a good hand, but in playing a poor hand well."

Denis Waitley (1933 -)

Motivational speaker

353

"A successful man is built of 1,000 failures."

Ray Allen (1975-)

Basketball player

354

"Do you want to know who you are? Don't ask. Act! Action will delineate and define you."

Thomas Jefferson (1743- 1826)

3rd U. S. President

355

"Success is the child of drudgery and perseverance. It cannot be coaxed or bribed; pay the price and it is yours."

Orison Swett Marden (1848- 1924)

Author

356

"With the new day comes new strength and new thoughts."

Eleanor Roosevelt (1884 - 1962)

Former First Lady of the United States

357

"To be successful you have to be lucky, or a little mad, or very talented, or find yourself in a rapid growth field."

Edward de Bono (1933 -)

Physician

358

"If your ship doesn't come in, swim out to meet it!"

Jonathan Winters (1925 - 2013)

Comedian

359

"A creative man is motivated by the desire to achieve, not by the desire to beat others."

Ayn Rand (1905 - 1982)

Writer

360

"Problems are not stop signs, they are guidelines."

Robert H. Schuller (1926 - 2015)

Televangelist

361

"I'm very competitive, and my ego couldn't handle that lack of success."

Gavin DeGraw (1977 -)

Musician

362

"If you don't design your own life plan, chances are you'll fall into someone else's plan. And guess what they have planned for you? Not much."

Jim Rohn (1930 - 2009)

Entrepreneur

363

"Passion is energy. Feel the power that comes from focusing on what excites you."

Oprah Winfrey (1954 -)

Host of The Oprah Winfrey Show

364

"You've got to follow your passion. You've got to figure out what it is you love -- who you really are. And have the courage to do that. I believe that the only courage anybody ever needs is the courage to follow your own dreams."

Oprah Winfrey (1954 -)

Host of The Oprah Winfrey Show

365

"If you think you can do it, you can."

John Burroughs (1837-)

Essayist

366

"Really liking what you do, whatever area that you get into, even if you're the best of the best, there's always a chance of failure. So, I think it's important that you really like whatever you're doing, if you don't like it, life is too short. If you like what you're doing, you think about it even when you're not working, it's something that your mind is drawn to. And if you don't like it, you really just can't make it work."

Elon Musk (1971-)

CEO of SpaceX

367

"Don't be afraid to give up the good to go for the great."

John D. Rockefeller (1839 - 1937)

Business magnate

368

"Without an open-minded mind, you can never be a great success."

Martha Stewart (1941 -)

Businesswoman

369

"Motivation is what gets you started. Habit is what keeps you going."

Jim Ryun (1947 -)

Athlete

370

"If you are not willing to risk the usual, you will have to settle for the ordinary."

Jim Rohn (1930 - 2009)

Entrepreneur

371

"To succeed in life, you need three things: a wishbone, a backbone and a funnybone."

Reba McEntire (1955 -)

Singer

372

"Success in any endeavor depends on the degree to which it is an expression of your true self."

Ralph Marston (1907 -)

Football player

373

"It is always the simple that produces the marvelous."

Amelia Barr (1831 - 1919)

Novelist

374

"Keep your eyes on the stars, and your feet on the ground."

Theodore Roosevelt (1858 - 1919)

26th U. S. President

375

"You don't have to see the whole staircase, just take the first step."

Martin Luther King, Jr. (1929 - 1968)

Minister

376

"I learned that we can do anything, but we can't do everything... at least not at the same time. So think of your priorities not in terms of what activities you do, but when you do them. Timing is everything."

Dan Millman (1946 -)

Author

377

"People are the key to success or extraordinary success."

Azim Premji (1945 -)

Chairman of Wipro

378

"The number one reason people fail in life is because they listen to their friends, family, and neighbors."

Napoleon Hill (1883 - 1970)

Author

379

"If you think you can, you can. And if you think you can't, you're right."

Henry Ford (1863 - 1947)

Founder of Ford Motor Company

380

"I have learned, that if one advances confidently in the direction of his dreams, and endeavors to live the life he has imagined, he will meet with a success unexpected in common hours."

Henry David Thoreau (1817 - 1862)

Essayist

381

"There is nothing impossible to him who will try."

Alexander the Great (356 BC - 323 BC)

King

382

"I'm a success today because I had a friend who believed in me and I didn't have the heart to let him down."

Abraham Lincoln (1809 - 1865)

16th U. S. President

383

"Our philosophy is that we care about people first."

Mark Zuckerberg (1984 -)

CEO of Facebook

384

"Optimism is the faith that leads to achievement. Nothing can be done without hope and confidence."

Helen Keller (1880 - 1968)

Author

385

"I've missed more than 9,000 shots in my career. I've lost almost 300 games. 26 times I've been trusted to take the game winning shot and missed. I've failed over and over and over again in my life and that is why I succeed."

Michael Jordan (1963 -)

Basketball player

386

"Modesty should be typical of the success of a champion."

Major Taylor (1878 - 1932)

Cyclist

387

"Don't give up. Don't lose hope. Don't sell out."

Christopher Reeve (1952 - 2004)

Actor

388

"The ultimate aim of the ego is not to see something, but to be something."

Muhammad Iqbal (1877 - 1938)

Poet

389

"He conquers who endures."

Persius (34 AD - 62 AD)

Poet

390

"Your heaviest artillery will be your will to live. Keep that big gun going."

Norman Cousins (1915 - 1990)

Journalist

391

"The most glorious moments in your life are not the so-called days of success, but rather those days when out of dejection and despair you feel rise in you a challenge to life, and the promise of future accomplishments."

Gustave Flaubert (1821 - 1880)

Novelist

392

"Don't let the fear of losing be greater than the excitement of winning."

Robert Kiyosaki (1947 -)

Businessman

393

"Small opportunities are often the beginning of great enterprises."

Demosthenes (384 BC - 322 BC)

Statesman

394

"Rest satisfied with doing well, and leave others to talk of you as they please."

Pythagoras (570 BC - 495 BC)

Philosopher

395

"Always do your best. What you plant now, you will harvest later."

Og Mandino (1923 - 1996)

Author

396

"Those who are successful overcome their fears and take action. Those who aren't submit to their fears and live with regrets."

Jay-Z (1969 -)

Rapper

397

"Vision without execution is just hallucination."

Henry Ford (1863 - 1947)

Founder of Ford Motor Company

398

"The first requisite for success is the ability to apply your physical and mental energies to one problem incessantly without growing weary."

Charles Caleb Colton (1780 - 1832)

Cleric

399

"Amateurs sit and wait for inspiration, the rest of us just get up and go to work."

Stephen King (1947 -)

Writer

400

"Do not wait to strike till the iron is hot; but make it hot by striking."

William Butler Yeats (1865 - 1939)

Poet

401

"Decide what you want, decide what you are willing to exchange for it. Establish your priorities and go to work."

H. L. Hunt (1889 - 1974)

Political activist

402

"The reason most people never reach their goals is that they don't define them, or ever seriously consider them as believable or achievable. Winners can tell you where they are going, what they plan to do along the way, and who will be sharing the adventure with them."

Denis Watiley (1933 -)

Motivational speaker

403

"The most effective way to do it, is to do it."

Amelia Earhart (1897-)

Aviator

404

"The only way to do great work is to love what you do. if you haven't found it yet, keep looking. don't settle."

Steve Jobs (1955- 2011)

Co-founder, Chairman, and CEO of Apple Inc.

405

"Perseverance is the hard work you do after you get tired of doing the hard work you already did."

Newt Gingrich (1943 -)

Former Speaker of the U.S. House of Representatives

406

"There is no failure except in no longer trying."

Elbert Hubbard (1856 - 1915)

Writer

407

"The best years of your life are the ones in which you decide your problems are your own. You do not blame them on your mother, the ecology, or the president. You realize that you control your own destiny."

Albert Ellis (1913 - 2007)

Psychologist

408

"You can't expect to hit the jackpot if you don't put a few nickels in the machine."

Flip Wilson (1933 - 1998)

Comedian

409

"The secret of success is constancy to purpose."

Benjamin Disraeli (1804 - 1881)

Former British Prime Minister

410

"There are no gains without pains."

Benjamin Franklin (1706 - 1790)

Founding Father of the United States

411

"Some people want it to happen, some wish it would happen, others make it happen."

Michael Jordan (1963 -)

Basketball player

412

"Never was anything great achieved without danger."

Niccolò Machiavelli (1469 - 1527)

Diplomat

413

"If you're changing the world, you're working on important things. You're excited to get up in the morning."

Larry Page (1973 -)

CEO of Alphabet

414

"Either I will find a way, or I will make one."

Philip Sidney (1554 - 1586)

Poet

415

"Where there is a will, there is a way. If there is a chance in a million that you can do something, anything, to keep what you want from ending, do it. Pry the door open or, if need be, wedge your foot in that door and keep it open."

Pauline Kael (1919 - 2001)

Film critic

416

"It is better to create than to learn! Creating is the essence of life."

Julius Caesar (100 BC - 44 BC)

Politician and military general

417

"The key to success is to focus our conscious mind on things we desire, not things we fear."

Brian Tracy (1944 -)

Motivational speaker

418

"Look up at the stars and not down at your feet. Try to make sense of what you see, and wonder about what makes the universe exist. Be curious."

Stephen Hawking (1942 - 2018)

Theoretical physicist

419

"I never did anything worth doing by accident, nor did any of my inventions come indirectly through accident, except the phonograph. No, when I have fully decided that a result is worth getting, I go about it, and make trial after trial, until it comes."

Thomas Edison (1847 - 1931)

Inventor

420

"Winners are not afraid of losing. But losers are. Failure is part of the process of success. People who avoid failure also avoid success."

Robert T. Kiyosaki (1947 -)

Businessman

421

"Success is nothing more than a few simple disciplines, practiced every day."

Jim Rohn (1930 - 2009)

Entrepreneur

422

"I've always tried to go a step past wherever people expected me to end up."

Beverly Sills (1929 - 2007)

Operatic soprano

423

"Keep your friends for friendship, but work with the skilled and competent."

Robert Greene (1959 -)

Author

424

"When something is important enough, you do it even if the odds are not in your favor."

Elon Musk (1971-)

CEO of SpaceX

425

"I'm never pleased with anything, I'm a perfectionist, it's part of who I am."

Michael Jackson (1958 - 2009)

Singer-songwriter

426

"Identify your problems but give your power and energy to solutions."

Tony Robbins (1960-)

Entrepreneur

427

"A good plan violently executed now is better than a perfect plan executed next week."

George S. Patton (1885 - 1945)

Senior officer

428

"If you don't like how things are, change it! You're not a tree."

Jim Rohn (1930 - 2009)

Entrepreneur

429

"Press forward. Do not stop, do not linger in your journey, but strive for the mark set before you."

George Whitefield (1714 - 1770)

Minister

430

"Be careful, ever so careful, in trumpeting your own achievements, and always talk less about yourself than about other people. Modesty is generally preferable."

Robert Greene (1959-)

Author

431

"Faith in your own powers and confidence in your individual methods are essential to success."

Roderick Stevens (1967 -)

Cinematographer

432

"Put your heart, mind, and soul into even your smallest acts. This is the secret of success."

Swami Sivananda (1887- 1963)

Teacher

433

"Whatever you want in life, other people are going to want it too. Believe in yourself enough to accept the idea that you have an equal right to it."

Diane Sawyer (1945 -)

Television journalist

434

"You must expect great things of yourself before you can do them."

Michael Jordan (1963 -)

Basketball player

435

"The universe doesn't give you what you ask for with your thoughts - it gives you what you demand with your actions."

Steve Maraboli (1975 -)

Researcher

436

"The secret of success is constancy of purpose."

Benjamin Disraeli (1804 - 1881)

Former British Prime Minister

437

"Know or listen to those who know."

Baltasar Gracian (1601 - 1658)

Prose writer

438

"Things work out best for those who make the best of how things work out."

John Wooden (1910 - 2010)

Basketball player

439

"Understanding the difference between healthy striving and perfectionism is critical to laying down the shield and picking up your life. Research shows that perfectionism hampers success. In fact, it's often the path to depression, anxiety, addiction, and life paralysis."

Brené Brown (1965 -)

Researcher

440

"Poverty was the greatest motivating factor in my life."

Jimmy Dean (1928 - 2010)

Singer

441

"Success is determined not by whether or not you face obstacles, but by your reaction to them. And if you look at these obstacles as a containing fence, they become your excuse for failure. If you look at them as a hurdle, each one strengthens you for the next."

Ben Carson (1951-)

17th United States Secretary of Housing and Urban Development

442

"As a general rule, the most successful man in life is the man who has the best information."

Benjamin Disraeli (1804- 1881)

Former British Prime Minister

443

"If you care about what you do and work hard at it, there isn't anything you can't do if you want to."

Jim Henson (1936- 1990)

Puppeteer

444

"Do not wait; the time will never be 'just right.' Start where you stand, and work with whatever tools you may have at your command, and better tools will be found as you go along."

George Herbert (1593 - 1633)

Poet

445

"The successful man is the one who had the chance and took it."

Roger Babson (1875 - 1967)

Entrepreneur

446

"Early in my career, I struggled with consistency, but I couldn't get more consistent than this year."

Roger Federer (1981 -)

Tennis player

447

"One important key to success is self-confidence. An important key to self-confidence is preparation."

Arthur Ashe (1943 - 1993)

Tennis player

448

"If you can dream it, you can do it."

Walt Disney (1901 - 1966)

Entrepreneur

449

"The secret of getting ahead is getting started."

Mark Twain (1835 - 1910)

Writer

450

"I know the price of success: dedication, hard work, and an unremitting devotion to the things you want to see happen."

Frank Lloyd Wright (1867 - 1959)

Architect

451

"There's a way to do it better - find it."

Thomas A. Edison (1847 - 1931)

Inventor

452

"Never retreat. Never explain. Get it done and let them howl."

Benjamin Jowett (1817 - 1893)

Academic

453

"Pursue one great decisive aim with force and determination."

Carl von Clausewitz (1780 - 1831)

General

454

"The two most powerful warriors are patience and time. So remember: great achievements take time, there is no overnight success."

Leo Tolstoy (1828 - 1910)

Novelist

455

"A dream you dream alone is only a dream. A dream you dream together is reality."

John Lennon (1940 - 1980)

Singer-songwriter

456

"Success is no accident. It is hard work, perseverance, learning, studying, sacrifice and most of all, love of what you are doing or learning to do."

Pele (1940 -)

Footballer

457

"I was motivated to be different in part because I was different."

Donna Brazile (1959 -)

Political strategist

458

"There is only one corner of the universe you can be certain of improving, and that's your own self."

Aldous Huxley (1894 - 1963)

Writer

459

"Follow effective actions with quiet reflection. From the quiet reflection will come even more effective action."

Peter Drucker (1909 - 2005)

Management consultant

460

"Doing the best at this moment puts you in the best place for the mext moment."

Oprah Winfrey (1954 -)

Host of The Oprah Winfrey Show

461

"Do whatever you do intensely."

Robert Henri (1865 - 1929)

Painter

462

"Do what you can with all you have, wherever you are."

Theodore Roosevelt (1858 - 1919)

26th U. S. President

463

"The most important single ingredient in the formula of success is knowing how to get along with people."

Theodore Roosevelt (1858 - 1919)

26th U. S. President

464

"The successful warrior is the average man, with laser-like focus."

Bruce Lee (1940 - 1973)

Martial artist

465

"In my experience, there is only one motivation, and that is desire. No reasons or principle contain it or stand against it."

Jane Smiley (1949-)

Novelist

466

"If you can't make it good, at least make it look good."

Bill Gates (1955-)

Business magnate

467

"All you need is the plan, the road map, and the courage to press on to your destination."

Earl Nightingale (1921- 1989)

Author

468

"I planned my success. I knew it was going to happen."

Erykah Badu (1971-)

Musician

469

"Start where you are. Use what you have. Do what you can."

Arthur Ashe (1943 - 1993)

Tennis player

470

"The way to get started is to quit talking and begin doing."

Walt Disney (1901 - 1966)

Entrepreneur

471

"Arriving at one goal is the starting point to another."

John Dewey (1859 - 1952)

Philosopher

472

"It is common sense to take a method and try it. If it fails, admit it frankly and try another. But above all, try something."

Franklin D. Roosevelt (1882 - 1945)

32nd U.S. President

473

"To each there comes in their lifetime a special moment when they are figuratively tapped on the shoulder and offered the chance to do a very special thing, unique to them and fitted to their talents. What a tragedy if that moment finds them unprepared or unqualified for that which could have been their finest hour."

Winston S. Churchill (1874 - 1965)

Former British Prime Minister

474

"It's how you deal with failure that determines how you achieve success."

Charlotte Whitton (1896 - 1975)

Former Mayor of Ottawa

475

"Making your mark on the world is hard. If it were easy, everybody would do it. But it's not. It takes patience, it takes commitment, and it comes with plenty of failure along the way. The real test is not whether you avoid this failure, because you won't. It's whether you let it harden or shame you into inaction, or whether you learn from it; whether you choose to persevere."

Barack Obama (1961 -)

44th U. S. President

476

"Take up one idea. Make that one idea your life - think of it, dream of it, live on that idea. Let the brain, muscles, nerves, every part of your body, be full of that idea, and just leave every other idea alone. This is the way to success."

Swami Vivekananda (1863 - 1902)

Indian monk

477

"You must take action now that will move you towards your goals. Develop a sense of urgency in your life."

H. Jackson Brown, Jr. (1940-)

Author

478

"You have to fight to reach your dream. You have to sacrifice and work hard for it."

Lionel Messi (1987-)

Footballer

479

"A man can be as great as he wants to be. If you believe in yourself and have the courage, the determination, the dedication, the competitive drive and if you are willing to sacrifice the little things in life and pay the price for the things that are worthwhile, it can be done."

Vince Lombardi (1913 - 1970)

Football player

480

"To begin, begin."

William Wordsworth (1770 - 1850)

Poet

481

"Pick battles big enough to matter, small enough to win."

Jonathan Kozol (1936 -)

Writer

482

"Without hard work, nothing grows but weeds."

Gordon B. Hinckley (1910 - 2008)

Religious leader

483

"I can, therefore I am."

Simone Weil (1909 - 1943)

Philosopher

484

"Set yourself earnestly to see what you are made to do, and then set yourself earnestly to do it."

Phillips Brooks (1835 - 1893)

Clergyman

485

"Things do not happen. Things are made to happen."

John F. Kennedy (1917 - 1963)

35th U. S. President

486

"I've had great success being a total idiot."

Jerry Lewis (1926 - 2017)

Comedian

487

"The successful man will profit from his mistakes and try again in a different way."

Dale Carnegie (1888 - 1955)

Writer

488

"No! Try not. Do, or do not. There is no try."

George Lucas (1944 -)

Filmmaker

489

"Give me a stock clerk with a goal and I'll give you a man who will make history. Give me a man with no goals and I'll give you a stock clerk."

J. C. Penney (1875 - 1971)

Founder of JCPenney

490

"Success isn't always going to be a huge contract; success is going to be if you just live out your purpose in life."

Allan Houston (1971-)

Basketball player

491

"When you show yourself to the world and display your talents, you naturally stir all kinds of resentment, envy, and other manifestations of insecurity... you cannot spend your life worrying about the petty feelings of others."

Robert Greene (1959-)

Author

492

"The first principle of success is desire – knowing what you want. Desire is the planting of your seed."

Robert Collier (1885 - 1950)

Author

493

"If you are working on something that you really care about, you don't have to be pushed. The vision pulls you."

Steve Jobs (1955 - 2011)

Co-founder, Chairman, and CEO of Apple Inc.

494

"If you do build a great experience, customers tell each other about that. Word of mouth is very powerful."

Jeff Bezos (1964 -)

CEO of Amazon

495

"You don't have to be great to start, but you have to start to be great."

Zig Ziglar (1926 - 2012)

Salesman

496

"One secret of success in life is for a man to be ready for his opportunity when it comes."

Benjamin Disraeli (1804 - 1881)

Former British Prime Minister

497

"If you try a bunch of things, you often learn more from failure than success."

Elon Musk (1971 -)

CEO of SpaceX

498

"Success seems to be connected with action. Successful people keep moving. They make mistakes, but they don't quit."

Conrad Hilton (1887 - 1979)

Hotel manager

499

"I failed my way to success."

Thomas Edison (1847 - 1931)

Inventor

500

"Success is the sum of small efforts – repeated day in and day out."

Robert Collier (1885 - 1950)

Author

501

"Successful and unsuccessful people do not vary greatly in their abilities. They vary in their desires to reach their potential."

John Maxwell (1947 -)

Author

502

"Talent is cheaper than table salt. What separates the talented individual from the successful one is a lot of hard work."

Stephen King (1947 -)

Writer

503

"Easy is not a option.. No days off.. Never Quit.. Be Fearless.. Talent you have Naturally.. Skill is only developed by hours and hours of work."

Usain Bolt (1986 -)

Olympic athlete

504

"Often it's the little, daily decisions – the ones you make hour by hour – that mean the difference between success and failure."

Mary Kay Ash (1918 - 2001)

Founder of Mary Kay Cosmetics

505

"One may miss the mark by aiming too high as too low."

Thomas Fuller (1608 - 1661)

Churchman

506

"He that succeeds makes an important thing of the immediate task."

William Feather (1889 - 1981)

Publisher

507

"The heights by great men reached and kept, were not attained by sudden flight, but they, while their companions slept, were toiling upward in the night."

Henry Wadsworth Longfellow (1807 - 1882)

Poet

508

"Always bear in mind that your own resolution to succeed is more important than any other one thing."

Abraham Lincoln (1809 - 1865)

16th U. S. President

509

"To be independent of public opinion is the first formal condition of achieving anything great."

Georg Wilhelm Friedrich Hegel (1770 - 1831)

Philosopher

510

"You don't have to start from scratch to do something interesting."

Jack Dorsey (1976 -)

CEO of Twitter Inc.

511

"I'm a very positive thinker, and I think that is what helps me the most in difficult moments."

Roger Federer (1981 -)

Tennis player

512

"Do your best when no one is looking. If you do that, then you can be successful in anything that you put your mind to."

Bob Cousy (1928 -)

Basketball player

513

"In order to succeed, we must first believe that we can."

Nikos Kazantzakis (1883 - 1957)

Poet

514

"I've always believed that if you put in the work, the results will come."

Michael Jordan (1963 -)

Basketball player

515

"By failing to prepare, you are preparing to fail."

Benjamin Franklin (1706 - 1790)

Founding Father of the United States

516

"People say to me, You were a roaring success. How did you do it? I go back to what my parents taught me. Apply yourself. Get all the education you can, but then, by God, do something. Don't just stand there, make something happen."

Lee Iacocca (1924-)

Businessman

517

"The doers are the major thinkers. The people that really create the things that change this industry are both the doer/thinker in one person."

Steve Jobs (1955-2011)

Co-founder, Chairman, and CEO of Apple Inc.

518

"The three great essentials to achieve anything worthwhile are, first, hard work; second, stick-to-itiveness; third, common sense."

Thomas A. Edison (1847-1931)

Inventor

519

"All we have to decide is what to do with the time that is given to us."

J. R. R. Tolkien (1892 - 1973)

Writer

520

"If you want to conquer fear, don't sit home and think about it. Go out and get busy."

Dale Carnegie (1888 - 1955)

Writer

521

"Either you run the day or the day runs you."

Jim Rohn (1930 - 2009)

Entrepreneur

522

"I find that the harder I work, the more luck I seem to have."

Thomas Jefferson (1743 - 1826)

3rd U. S. President

523

"When you do the common things in life in an uncommon way, you will command the attention of the world."

George Washington Carver (1860s - 1943)

Botanist

524

"Definiteness of purpose is the starting point of all achievement."

W. Clement Stone (1902 - 2002)

Businessman

525

"When one must, one can."

Charlotte Whitton (1896 - 1975)

Former Mayor of Ottawa

526

"You can't wait for inspiration. You have to go after it with a club."

Jack London (1876 - 1916)

Novelist

527

"Everything I've ever done was out of fear of being mediocre."

Chet Atkins (1924 - 2001)

Musician

528

"Good, better, best. Never let it rest. 'Til your good is better and your better is best."

St. Jerome (347 AD - 420 AD)

Priest

529

"The first man gets the oyster, the second man gets the shell."

Andrew Carnegie (1835 - 1919)

Industrialist

530

"If you want to be the best, you have to do things that other people aren't willing to do."

Michael Phelps (1985 -)

Swimmer

531

"Always desire to learn something useful."

Sophocles (?- 406 BC)

Tragedian

532

"Flaming enthusiasm, backed up by horse sense and persistence, is the quality that most frequently makes for success."

Dale Carnegie (1888 - 1955)

Writer

533

"To be successful be ahead of your time, but only a little."

Mason Cooley (1927 - 2002)

Aphorist

534

"Action is the foundational key to all success."

Pablo Picasso (1881 - 1973)

Painter

535

"Develop success from failures. Discouragement and failure are two of the surest stepping stones to success."

Dale Carnegie (1888 - 1955)

Writer

536

"In most things success depends on knowing how long it takes to succeed."

Montesquieu (1689 - 1755)

Philosopher

537

"Perseverance – a lowly virtue whereby mediocrity achieves an inglorious success."

Ambrose Bierce (1842 - 1914)

Short story writer

538

"Little by little, one travels far."

J. R. R. Tolkien (1892 - 1973)

Writer

539

"Success follows doing what you want to do. There is no other way to be successful."

Malcolm Forbes (1919 - 1990)

Publisher

540

"Singleness of purpose is essential for success in life."

John D. Rockefeller (1839 - 1937)

Business magnate

541

"Fortune sides with him who dares."

Virgil (70 BC - 19 BC)

Poet

542

"Your talent is God's gift to you. What you do with it is your gift back to God."

Leo Buscaglia (1924 - 1998)

Motivational speaker

543

"Successful people are 100% convinced that they are masters of their own destiny, they're not creatures of circumstance, they create circumstance, if the circumstances around them suck they change them."

Jordan Belfort (1962 -)

Author

544

"All of us every single year, we're a different person. I don't think we're the same person all our lives."

Steven Spielberg (1946 -)

Filmmaker

545

"It does not matter how slowly you go as long as you do not stop."

Confucius (551 BC - 479 BC)

Chinese teacher

546

"I always tried to turn every disaster into an opportunity."

John D. Rockefeller (1839 - 1937)

Business magnate

547

"Talent without working hard is nothing."

Cristiano Ronaldo (1985 -)

Footballer

548

"To become an able and successful man in any profession, three things are necessary, nature, study and practice."

Henry Ward Beecher (1813 - 1887)

Protestant Clergyman

549

"Success is not the key to happiness. Happiness is the key to success. If you love what you are doing, you will be successful."

Albert Schweitzer (1875 - 1965)

Theologian

550

"I have always observed that to succeed in the world one should appear like a fool but be wise."

Montesquieu (1689 - 1755)

Philosopher

551

"The young do not know enough to be prudent, and therefore they attempt the impossible – and achieve it, generation after generation."

Pearl S. Buck (1892 - 1973)

Writer

552

"Recipe for success: Be polite, prepare yourself for whatever you are asked to do, keep yourself tidy, be cheerful, don't be envious, be honest with yourself so you will be honest with others, be helpful, interest yourself in your job, don't pity yourself, be quick to praise, be loyal to your friends, avoid prejudices, be independent, interest yourself in politics, and read the newspapers."

Bernard M. Baruch (1870 - 1965)

Financier

553

"To be successful you need friends and to be very successful you need enemies."

Sidney Sheldon (1917 - 2007)

Novelist

554

"The only question to ask yourself is, how much are you willing to sacrifice to achieve this success?"

Larry Flynt (1942-)

Publisher

555

"There is a powerful driving force inside every human being that, once unleashed, can make any vision, dream, or desire a reality."

Anthony Robbins (1960-)

Entrepreneur

556

"The key to success is to keep growing in all areas of life – mental, emotional, spiritual, as well as physical."

Julius Erving (1950-)

Basketball player

557

"Failure is the key to success; each mistake teaches us something."

Morihei Ueshiba (1883 - 1969)

Martial artist

558

"We can be truly successful only at something we're willing to fail at."

Mark Manson (1984 -)

Writer

559

"We aim above the mark to hit the mark."

Ralph Waldo Emerson (1803 - 1882)

Essayist

560

"So be sure when you step, Step with care and great tact. And remember that life's A Great Balancing Act. And will you succeed? Yes! You will, indeed! (98 and ¾ percent guaranteed) Kid, you'll move mountains."

Dr. Seuss (1904 - 1991)

Writer

561

"Success is a science; if you have the conditions, you get the result."

Oscar Wilde (1854 - 1900)

Author

562

"Self-trust is the first secret of success."

Ralph Waldo Emerson (1803 - 1882)

Essayist

563

"I gave up a lot of things in exchange for my success."

Billy Sheehan (1953 -)

Musician

564

"Your time is limited, so don't waste it living someone else's life."

Steve Jobs (1955 - 2011)

Co-founder, Chairman, and CEO of Apple Inc.

565

"I'm tough, I'm ambitious, and I know exactly what I want. If that makes me a bitch, okay."

Madonna (1958 -)

Singer-songwriter

566

"Your chances of success in any undertaking can always be measured by your belief in yourself."

Robert Collier (1885 - 1950)

Author

567

"Infuse your life with action. Don't wait for it to happen. Make it happen. Make your own future. Make your own hope. Make your own love. And whatever your beliefs, honor your creator, not by passively waiting for grace to come down from upon high, but by doing what you can to make grace happen... yourself, right now, right down here on Earth."

Bradley Whitford (1959 -)

Actor

568

"Only those who dare to fail greatly can ever achieve greatly."

Robert F. Kennedy (1925 - 1968)

Former United States Senator

569

"There are no secrets to success. It is the result of preparation, hard work, and learning from failure."

Colin Powell (1937 -)

Former United States National Security Advisor

570

"If you really look closely, most overnight successes took a long time."

Steve Jobs (1955 - 2011)

Co-founder, Chairman, and CEO of Apple Inc.

571

"**Setting goals is the first step in turning the invisible into the visible.**"

Tony Robbins (1960 -)

Entrepreneur

572

"**All men seek one goal: success or happiness. The only way to achieve true success is to express yourself completely in service to society. First, have a definite, clear, practical ideal-a goal, an objective. Second, have the necessary means to achieve your ends-wisdom, money, materials and methods. Third, adjust all your means to that end.**"

Aristotle (384 BC - 322 BC)

Philosopher

573

"The professional has learned that success, like happiness, comes as a by-product of work. The professional concentrates on the work and allows rewards to come or not come, whatever they like."

Steven Pressfield (1943 -)

Author

574

"I've found that luck is quite predictable. If you want more luck, take more chances. Be more active. Show up more often."

Brian Tracy (1944 -)

Motivational speaker

SUCCESS: *Keeping Positive*

575

"Whenever you're in conflict with someone, there is one factor that can make the difference between damaging your relationship and deepening it. That factor is attitude."

William James (1842 - 1910)

Philosopher

576

"You are never too old to set another goal or to dream a new dream."

Les Brown (1945 -)

Author

577

"When everything seems to be going against you, remember that the airplane takes off against the wind, not with it."

Henry Ford (1863 - 1947)

Founder of Ford Motor Company

578

"Optimism is the faith that leads to achievement."

Helen Keller (1880 - 1968)

Author

579

"Done is better than perfect."

Sheryl Sandberg (1969 -)

COO of Facebook

580

"Follow your heart. Don't follow what you've been told you're supposed to do."

J. Cole (1985 -)

Hip-hop artist

581

"Dark and difficult times lie ahead. Soon we must all face the choice between what is right and what is easy."

J. K. Rowling (1965-)

Novelist

582

"You always pass failure on the way to success."

Mickey Rooney (1920- 2014)

Actor

583

"Each day provides its own gifts."

Marcus Aurelius (121 AD- 180 AD)

Roman emperor

584

"If you're going through hell, keep going."

Winston Churchill (1874 - 1965)

Former British Prime Minister

585

"Every exit is an entry somewhere else."

Tom Stoppard (1937 -)

Playwright

586

"Keep your face always toward the sunshine—and shadows will fall behind you."

Walt Whitman (1819 - 1892)

Poet

587

"Today is cruel. Tomorrow is crueller. And the day after tomorrow is beautiful."

Jack Ma (1964 -)

Founder and Executive Chairman of Alibaba Group

588

"Don't let the noise of others' opinions drown out your own inner voice. And most important, have the courage to follow your heart and intuition. They somehow already know what you truly want to become. Everything else is secondary."

Steve Jobs (1955 - 2011)

Co-founder, Chairman, and CEO of Apple Inc.

589

"Success is sweet and sweeter if long delayed and gotten through many struggles and defeats."

Amos Bronson Alcott (1799 - 1888)

Educator

590

"It doesn't matter how slowly you go – as long as you don't stop!"

Confucius (551 BC - 479 BC)

Chinese teacher

591

"The expert in anything was once a beginner."

Helen Hayes (1900 - 1993)

Actress

592

"Little minds are tamed and subdued by misfortune; but great minds rise above it."

Washington Irving (1783 - 1859)

Short story writer

593

"Fortune always favors the brave, and never helps a man who does not help himself."

P. T. Barnum (1810 - 1891)

Showman

594

"To see what is right and not do it is a lack of courage."

Confucious (551 BC - 479 BC)

Chinese teacher

595

"Whatever the mind can conceive and believe, it can achieve."

Napoleon Hill (1883 - 1970)

Author

596

"No-one knows what he can do until he tries."

Publilius Syrus (85 BC - 43 BC)

Writer

597

"The best way to gain self-confidence is to do what you are afraid to do."

Swati Sharma (1973 -)

Playback singer

598

"Don't think of it as failure. Think of it as time-released success."

Robert Orben (1927 -)

Writer

599

"There are far, far better things ahead than any we leave behind."

C.S. Lewis (1898 - 1963)

Novelist

600

"Big shots are only little shots who keep shooting."

Christopher Morley (1890 - 1957)

Journalist

601

"Security is mostly a superstition. Life is either a daring adventure or nothing."

Helen Keller (1880 - 1968)

Author

602

"Doubt kills more dreams than failure ever will."

Suzy Kassem (1975 -)

Writer

603

"Most of the important things in the world have been accomplished by people who have kept on trying when there seemed to be no help at all."

Dale Carnegie (1888 - 1955)

Writer

604

"Optimism is the one quality more associated with success and happiness than any other."

Brian Tracy (1944 -)

Motivational speaker

605

"Our greatest glory is not in never falling, but in rising every time we fall."

Oliver Goldsmith (1728 - 1774)

Playwright

606

"A year from now you may wish you had started today."

Karen Lamb (1956 -)

Author

607

"The question isn't who is going to let me; it's who is going to stop me."

Ayn Rand (1905 - 1982)

Writer

608

"Nothing is impossible, the word itself says 'I'm possible'!"

Audrey Hepburn (1929 - 1993)

Actress

609

"Before success comes in any man's life, he's sure to meet with much temporary defeat and, perhaps some failures. When defeat overtakes a man, the easiest and the most logical thing to do is to quit. That's exactly what the majority of men do."

Napoleon Hill (1883 - 1970)

Author

610

"It is never too late to be what you might have been."

George Eliot (1819 - 1880)

Novelist

611

"Sometimes life is going to hit you in the head with a brick. Don't lose faith."

Steve Jobs (1955 - 2011)

Co-founder, Chairman, and CEO of Apple Inc.

612

"Sometimes life knocks you on your ass... get up, get up, get up!!! Happiness is not the absence of problems, it's the ability to deal with them."

Steve Maraboli (1975 -)

Researcher

613

"If you believe it will work out, you'll see opportunities. If you believe it won't, you will see obstacles."

Wayne Dyer (1940 - 2015)

Teacher

614

"Before success comes in any man's life, he is sure to meet with much temporary defeat, and, perhaps, some failure. When defeat overtakes a man, the easiest and most logical thing to do is to quit. That is exactly what the majority of men do. More than five hundred of the most successful men this country has ever known told the author their greatest success came just one step beyond the point at which defeat had overtaken them."

Napoleon Hill (1883 - 1970)

Author

615

"You must be the change you wish to see in the world."

Mahatma Gandhi (1869 - 1948)

Lawyer

616

"Once we believe in ourselves, we can risk curiosity, wonder, spontaneous delight, or any experience that reveals the human spirit."

E. E. Cummings (1894 - 1962)

Author

617

"You just can't beat the person who never gives up."

Babe Ruth (1895 -)

Baseball player

618

"Behind every successful man there's a lot of unsuccessful years."

Bob Brown (1944 -)

General practitioner

619

"The more that you read, the more things you will know. The more you learn, the more places you'll go!"

Dr. Seuss (1904 - 1991)

Writer

620

"I had a lot of failure. I failed for, funny things that I failed in, a key primary school test for two times. I failed three times for the middle schools. You know for three years I tried, failed in the universities. So I applied jobs for thirty times, got rejected. I went for the police, they said, "No you're not good." I went to even the KFC, when KFC came to China, came to our city, people went for the job. Twenty-three people accepted. I was the only one who got rejected. We went for police, five people, four of them accepted. I was the only guy they did not proceed with. So to me, being turned down, rejected — oh by the way, I told you that I applied for Harvard, ten times, rejected. I knew I'd be rejected, I just wanted to see."

Jack Ma (1964 -)

Founder and Executive Chairman of Alibaba Group

621

"You're braver than you believe, and stronger than you seem, and smarter than you think."

A.A. Milne (1882 - 1956)

Novelist

622

"Remembering that you are going to die is the best way I know to avoid the trap of thinking you have something to lose. You are already naked. There is no reason not to follow your heart."

Steve Jobs (1955 - 2011)

Cofounder, Chairman, and CEO of Apple Inc.

623

"Many of life's failures are people who did not realize how close they were to success when they gave up."

Thomas Edison (1847 - 1931)

Inventor

624

"If you fell down yesterday, stand up today."

H. G. Wells (1866 - 1946)

Novelist

625

"All my growth and development led me to believe that if you really do the right thing, and if you play by the rules, and if you've got good enough, solid judgment and common sense, that you're going to be able to do whatever you want to do with your life."

Barbara Jordan (1936 - 1996)

Lawyer

626

"That some achieve great success, is proof to all that others can achieve it as well."

Abraham Lincoln (1809 - 1865)

16th U. S. President

627

"Our greatest weakness lies in giving up. The most certain way to succeed is always to try just one more time."

Thomas A. Edison (1847 - 1931)

Inventor

628

"Believe you can and you're halfway there."

Theodore Roosevelt (1858 - 1919)

26th U. S. President

629

"If you don't risk anything, you risk even more."

Erica Jong (1942 -)

Author and teacher

630

"Don't let yesterday take up too much of today."

Will Rogers (1879 - 1935)

Comedic actor

631

"What seems to us as bitter trials are often blessings in disguise."

Oscar Wilde (1854 - 1900)

Author

632

"Perseverance is failing 19 times and succeeding the 20th."

Julie Andrews (1935 -)

Actress

633

"Failure is the condiment that gives success its flavor."

Truman Capote (1924 - 1984)

Artist

634

"The pessimist sees difficulty in every opportunity. The optimist sees opportunity in every difficulty."

Winston Churchill (1874 - 1965)

Former British Prime Minister

635

"The road to success is always under construction."

Lily Tomlin (1939 -)

Actress

636

"There is only one thing that makes a dream impossible to achieve: the fear of failure."

Paulo Coelho (1947-)

Lyricist and novelist

637

"If you really want to do something, you'll find a way. If you don't, you'll find an excuse."

Jim Rohn (1930-2009)

Entrepreneur

638

"The harder the conflict, the more glorious the triumph."

Thomas Paine (1737-1809)

Founding Father of the United States

639

"Everything you've ever wanted is on the other side of fear."

George Addair (1823 - 1899)

Real-estate developer

640

"It's not whether you get knocked down, it's whether you get up."

Vince Lombardi (1913 - 1970)

Football player

641

"It always seems impossible until it's done."

Nelson Mandela (1918 - 2013)

Activist

642

"A goal is a dream with a deadline."

Napoleon Hill (1883 - 1970)

Author

643

"Never, never, never give up."

Winston Churchill (1874 - 1965)

Former British Prime Minister

644

"Without failure there is no sweetness in success. There's no understanding of it."

Glenn Beck (1964 -)

Talk show host

645

"The only limit to our realization of tomorrow will be our doubts of today."

Franklin D. Roosevelt (1882 - 1945)

32nd U. S. President

646

"To be yourself in a world that is constantly trying to make you something else is the greatest accomplishment."

Ralph Waldo Emerson (1803 - 1882)

Essayist

647

"Life isn't about finding yourself. Life is about creating yourself."

George Bernard Shaw (1856 - 1950)

Playwright

648

"Hardships often prepare ordinary people for an extraordinary destiny."

C.S. Lewis (1898 - 1963)

Novelist

649

"No man ever achieved worth-while success who did not, at one time or other, find himself with at least one foot hanging well over the brink of failure."

Napoleon Hill (1883 - 1970)

Author

650

"Knowing what must be done does away with fear."

Rosa Parks (1913 - 2005)

Civil rights activist

651

**"Creativity is intelligence having fun.
"**

Albert Einstein (1879 - 1955)

Theoretical physicist

652

"I am not afraid... I was born to do this."

Joan of Arc (1412 - 1431)

Saint

653

"Real difficulties can be overcome; it is only the imaginary ones that are unconquerable."

Theodore N. Vail (1845 - 1920)

President of American Telephone & Telegraph

654

"I arise full of eagerness and energy, knowing well what achievement lies ahead of me."

Zane Grey (1872 - 1939)

Novelist

655

"Life shrinks or expands in proportion to one's courage."

Anais Nin (1903 - 1977)

Author

656

"Today's accomplishments were yesterday's impossibilities."

Robert H. Schuller (1926 - 2015)

Televangelist

657

"You can never quit. Winners never quit, and quitters never win."

Ted Turner (1938 -)

Founder of TBS and CNN

658

"You're going to go through tough times – that's life. But I say, 'Nothing happens to you, it happens for you.' See the positive in negative events."

Joel Osteen (1963 -)

Televangelist

659

"You may not realize it when it happens, but a kick in the teeth may be the best thing in the world for you."

Walt Disney (1901- 1966)

Entrepreneur

660

"A minute's success pays the failure of years."

Robert Browning (1812 - 1889)

Poet

661

"Inaction breeds doubt and fear. Action breeds confidence and courage. If you want to conquer fear, do not sit home and think about it. Go out and get busy."

Dale Carnegie (1888 - 1955)

Writer

662

"The ones who are crazy enough to think they can change the world, are the ones that do."

Steve Jobs (1955 - 2011)

Co-founder, Chairman, and CEO of Apple Inc.

663

"People often say that motivation doesn't last. Well, neither does bathing — that's why we recommend it daily."

Zig Ziglar (1926 - 2012)

Salesman

664

"Character cannot be developed in ease and quiet. Only through experience of trial and suffering can the soul be strengthened, ambition inspired, and success achieved."

Helen Keller (1880 - 1968)

Author

665

"Go confidently in the direction of your dreams. Live the life you have imagined."

Henry David Thoreau (1817 - 1862)

Essayist

666

"The best revenge is massive success."

Frank Sinatra (1915 - 1998)

Singer

667

"Nothing is particularly hard if you break it down into small jobs."

Henry Ford (1863 - 1947)

Founder of Ford Motor Company

668

"Believe in yourself and all that you are. Know that there is something inside you that is greater than any obstacle."

Christian D. Larson (1874 - 1954)

Author

669

"All our dreams can come true, if we have the courage to pursue them."

Walt Disney (1901 - 1966)

Entrepreneur

670

"Your time is limited, don't waste it living someone else's life. Don't be trapped by dogma, which is living the result of other people's thinking. Don't let the noise of other's opinion drowned your own inner voice. And most important, have the courage to follow your heart and intuition, they somehow already know what you truly want to become. Everything else is secondary."

Steve Jobs (1955 - 2011)

Cofounder, Chairman, and CEO of Apple Inc.

671

"Light tomorrow with today."

Elizabeth Barrett Browning (1806 - 1861)

Poet

672

"I think success has no rules, but you can learn a great deal from failure."

Jean Kerr (1922 - 2003)

Author

673

"Your attitude, not your aptitude, will determine your altitude."

Zig Ziglar (1926 - 2012)

Salesman

674

"Strength does not come from physical capacity. It comes from an indomitable will."

Mahatma Gandhi (1869 - 1948)

Lawyer

675

"Despite the successes, you remember the failures – rather lovingly."

Harold Prince (1928 -)

Theatrical producer

676

"When you reach the end of your rope, tie a knot in it and hang on."

Franklin D. Roosevelt (1882 - 1945)

32nd U. S. President

677

"A rejection is nothing more than a necessary step in the pursuit of success."

Bo Bennett (1972 -)

Author

678

"Never give up on what you really want to do. The person with big dreams is more powerful than one with all the facts."

Albert Einstein (1879 - 1955)

Theoretical physicist

679

"It is during our darkest moments that we must focus to see the light."

Aristotle Onassis (1906 - 1975)

Shipping tycoon

680

"Success is not built on success. It's built on failure. It's built on frustration. Sometimes it's built on catastrophe."

Navjot Singh Sidhu (1963 -)

Politician

681

"Whatever you hold in your mind on a consistent basis is exactly what you will experience in your life."

Tony Robbins (1960 -)

Entrepreneur

682

"We may encounter many defeats but we must not be defeated."

Maya Angelou (1928 - 2014)

Writer

683

"Always be yourself, express yourself, have faith in yourself, do not go out and look for a successful personality and duplicate it."

Bruce Lee (1940 - 1973)

Martial artist

684

"We got dreams and we got the right to chase 'em."

J. Cole (1985-)

Hip-hop artist

685

"It's always too early to quit."

Norman Vincent Peale (1898- 1993)

Minister

686

"Failure will never overtake me if my determination to succeed is strong enough."

Og Mandino (1923- 1996)

Author

687

"Believe in yourself, take on your challenges, dig deep within yourself to conquer fears. Never let anyone bring you down. You got to keep going."

Chantal Sutherland (1976 -)

Model

688

"Frustration, although quite painful at times, is a very positive and essential part of success."

Bo Bennett (1972 -)

Author

689

"If you hear a voice within you say 'you cannot paint,' then by all means paint, and that voice will be silenced."

Vincent Van Gogh (1853 - 1890)

Painter

690

"Let us make our future now, and let us make our dreams tomorrow's reality."

Malala Yousafzai (1997-)

Activist for female education

691

"Never limit yourself because of others' limited imagination; never limit others because of your own limited imagination."

Mae Jemison (1956-)

Engineer

692

"Be miserable. Or motivate yourself. Whatever has to be done, it's always your choice."

Wayne Dyer (1940-2015)

Teacher

693

"I have not failed. I've just found 10,000 ways that won't work."

Thomas A. Edison (1847 - 1931)

Inventor

694

"Limitations live only in our minds. But if we use our imaginations, our possibilities become limitless."

Jamie Paolinetti (1964 -)

Film director

695

"Most of the important things in the world have been accomplished by people who have kept on trying when there seemed to be no hope at all."

Dale Carnegie (1888 - 1955)

Writer

696

"I'm the most successful bad player ever."

Andy Roddick (1982-)

Tennis player